How to Make Probiotic Drinks for a l   :er, and
Naturally Fermen

By R.J. Ruppenthal, Attorney/Professor/Food and Garden Writer

1. Probiotic Foods for Better Health
Improve Digestion and Strengthen Your Immune System

2. The Benefits of Fermented Beverages
Lose Weight, Nourish Your Body, and Boost Energy Levels

3. Drinkable Yogurt
It's Easy, Quick to Make, and Tastes Great

4. Rejuvelac
The Goodness of Sprouted Grains in a Glass

5. SCOBIES: Ancient and Modern
The World's Most Natural, Complex Probiotic Cultures

6. Alcoholic Content of Fermented Beverages
Booze Content is Usually Less Than 1%, But Be Careful

7. Kefir: Milk and Water-Based Versions
The Secret to Longer Life?

8. Kombucha
Delicious and Healthful Beverage

9. Ginger Beer
Naturally Brewed With a Unique Culture

10. Home Brewed Ciders and Sodas
Bottle Your Own Naturally Effervescent Sodas in Any Flavor

11. Probiotic Smoothies
Drink Your Food…Delicious and Nutritious

12. Additional Recipes for Kombucha, Sodas, and Smoothies
Wait till you try some of these!

Chapter 1: Probiotic Foods for Better Health

This short book is a guide to making your own fermented, probiotic drinks. Using beneficial cultures, like the good bacteria in yogurt, you will learn how to create healthy, delicious drinks that benefit your body. For thousands of years, long before sugary soft drinks were invented, our ancestors enjoyed the whole food goodness of fermented drinks such as kefir, kombucha, and naturally fermented ciders and sodas. If delicious raw food smoothies were not around 5,000 years ago, it is only because our Stone Age ancestors did not have good blenders.

Fermented drinks are tasty, easy to prepare, and incredibly healthy. Yogurt, kefir, kombucha, and other probiotic drinks are made by adding cultures to base ingredients such as milk, sweet tea, or fruit juice. The cultures consist of beneficial microorganisms, such as Lactobacillus acidophilus, which add live enzymes, B vitamins, and protein to your food. Other probiotic raw foods, including cottage cheese, sauerkraut, kimchi, will be covered in an upcoming companion book.

In addition, the "good bacteria" make it easier for you to digest your food, helping your body to assimilate more nutrition and rid itself of toxins. Improved digestion is the most natural way to improve the radiance of your skin, keep your bowel movements regular, and help you sleep better. With less excess sugar and toxic waste, your body will find itself with a lot less work to do. Many people who add probiotics to their diets wake up feeling more vibrant, rejuvenated, and full of energy.

Along with these benefits often comes a loss of excess weight and an immune system that seems more resistant to invaders. While only a handful of scientific studies have measured the effects of probiotics on immune system health, individuals have used them to treat everything from cancer to the common cold. However, fermented foods are less of a medicine than a healthy addition to your diet. Eat and drink more of them, and you may provide your body with the stronger support it needs to resist diseases, infections, and other health problems.

Most health-related studies are funded by large corporations, particularly pharmaceutical giants. It costs a great deal of money to conduct a comprehensive study to test the health benefits of a certain food. Unfortunately, most large companies do not get too excited about testing foods that people can make or obtain easily. They are most interested in finding obscure substances they can turn into drugs and sell for large profits. This is the main reason that there are not more studies demonstrating the health benefits of fermented foods.

Chapter 2: The Benefits of Fermented Beverages

Raw food contains whole nutrition, some of which is destroyed in the cooking process. Up until about 12,000 years ago, our ancestors did not cook their food, so our bodies developed to accommodate raw food. The large quantities of cooked and over-processed food in the modern diet overwhelm the body's ability to digest and process all those substances. This probably contributes to high rates of cancer, diabetes, heart disease, and other chronic health problems.

You do not need to go full hog to enjoy the benefits of raw food. Just eat some yogurt or a salad. Including more raw foods in your diet can help restore energy levels and leave you feeling better.

I enjoy some cooked meals as much as the next person, but I have come to understand the importance of eating more raw foods as part of a balanced diet. Now, whenever I seat something that is cooked, I always eat it with live, cultured, fermented foods or drinks such as yogurt, sauerkraut, kombucha, or ginger beer.

Raw foods have their enzymes intact, making them easier for people to digest. Fermented foods are even healthier in this way. Their beneficial cultures supply additional enzymes to assist with digestion and other physical processes. Fermented foods are an essential part of any raw food diet.

While it is possible to make any of the beverages in this book by using a simple yeast culture (brewer's yeast, wine yeast, or baker's yeast), these yeasts are not strong probiotic cultures. This book describes the healthier traditional methods of using complex cultures of bacteria and yeasts to make delicious drinks that also carry strong probiotic properties. Studies have proven that, when it comes to probiotic cultures, strains matter. The strains of beneficial bacteria and yeasts that are in kefir, kombucha, and ginger beer plant cultures have been tested for their health benefits over a period of many centuries.

We will get to these complex cultures soon enough. First, we will cover two much simpler fermentation projects. The first is making yogurt and the second is making rejuvelac, a fermented beverage made from sprouted grains. Once you have made yogurt or rejuvelac, you can move on to the advanced level and try some other rewarding and healthful drinks: naturally fermented kefir, kombucha, and ginger beer, ciders, sodas, and more.

Before we continue, here is one quick note about using metallic materials. Most home fermenters avoid using metal pots, bowls, and utensils when working with natural cultures. This is because metal objects transmit small amounts of electricity. Theoretically, this could damage the beneficial organisms that make up the cultures.

Studies have failed to demonstrate any such effect, so you may choose to go on using metal objects. But if you prefer to be as cautious as most people, you should stick to non-metallic materials such as glass, plastic, or ceramic bowls and containers, wooden or plastic spoons, silicon spatulas, and so forth. Most people have these in their kitchens. The one item that most people do not have (and which is quite useful in a number of these recipes) is a non-metallic strainer. For just a few dollars, you can get a well made nylon strainer that can last for many years. Try an Amazon or Google search for "nylon strainer" or "plastic kefir strainer".

Chapter 3: Making Yogurt

Let's begin with yogurt, which is a well known fermented food that makes a healthy addition to one's diet. With its creamy, custardy texture, yogurt can serve as a lower calorie substitute for more fattening foods such as ice cream, pudding, whipped cream, and sour cream. It blends easily into smoothies and shakes (please see the chapter on smoothies for more on this). It combines well with fruit and cereal for an easy breakfast. You can even use yogurt in a savory dip or cold soup. There are an endless number of ways to incorporate yogurt into your meals.

Yogurt has been a popular health food for many years and its benefits have been widely reported. Though yogurt is milder than most probiotics, it is believed to provide many of the same benefits: better digestion, stronger immunity against diseases, detoxification, and the possibility of weight loss. Also, culturing milk with beneficial yogurt bacteria helps your body absorb its nutrients better. You will get more calcium, protein, and B vitamins (to name a few) from eating yogurt than from drinking the milk it was cultured in.

You can make yogurt in just a few hours with just milk and starter cultures. Alternatively, you can use a non-dairy milk such as rice milk, coconut milk, or almond milk (soy milk works, too, but it is trickier to culture). To inoculate your milk with good bacteria, start with freeze dried yogurt starter or a few ounces of high quality yogurt that has active cultures. We will cover the process after taking a closer look at the good bacteria in yogurt.

Most yogurt in the United States is cultured with no more than four strains of bacteria: *Lactobacillus bulgaricus, Streptococcus thermophilus, Lactobacillus acidophilus, and Lactobacillus bifidus*. However, two of these cultures cannot survive the journey into your digestive tract, while the other two probably will not arrive in sufficient numbers to make a meaningful difference your digestive tract. For these reasons, some of the premier yogurt brands (like Stonyfield, Green Valley, and Nancy's) include some additional cultures that have been proven to help build immunity, such as *Lactobacillus casei, Lactobacillus reuteri,* and *Lactobacillus rhamnosus.*

Below is a 1970s ad for Dannon Yogurt (TM). It is a bit blurry to read, so here's the punch line. At the top, it says, "Dannon Yogurt may not help you live as long as Soviet Georgians. But it couldn't hurt." The captions on the pictures read (at left) "Bagrat Topagua, Age 89" and (at right) "His mother." Of course, this region is the birthplace of kefir as well, which we will cover here shortly.

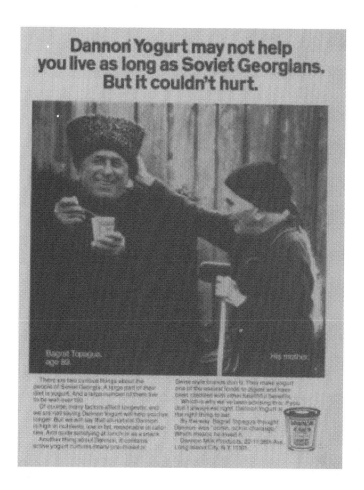

Yogurt

(If you have a yogurt maker, then follow the directions that came with your machine; this recipe is designed for someone who does not have a yogurt maker)

You can make yogurt at room temperature, but the cultures do their job better in warmer temperatures (up to about 100 F degrees, since much hotter than this will kill them). These directions show you how to make yogurt using an oven, a heating pad, a slow cooker or crock pot, and a warm water bath.

Recipe makes one quart of drinkable, European-style yogurt. Below are two variations.

Solid, American-style yogurt: If you prefer solid yogurt, then heat the milk first in a pot on the stove until it comes to a boil, turn off heat and let it cool to below 100 F degrees. Then follow the same directions below. Boiling the milk first makes a solid yogurt, while not boiling it makes a more liquid yogurt.

Greek-style yogurt: Make the solid yogurt above and follow the basic yogurt making directions below. Then place your solid yogurt in a strainer over a bowl, cover it with a towel, and let the liquid drain out for a few hours. If your strainer has large holes, then line it with a couple of paper towels first. You can use the liquid whey to culture rejuvelac, cider, soda, and other fermented drinks, while the solid yogurt that remains will taste better than any Greek yogurt from the store.

Required materials:
One quart-sized container, such as a glass jar, plastic container, or glass or ceramic bowl
One kitchen towel to cover the container
One large mixing bowl (glass, plastic, or ceramic)
One wooden spoon, silicon spatula, or other non-metal utensil
Optional: One cooking thermometer or cheese thermometer

Ingredients:
One quart of milk (NOT ultra-pasteurized milk, which does not culture well)
One quarter cup or one half cup of plain yogurt (choose a good one which contains active cultures). Or you can use powdered yogurt culture, available from health food stores.

Process:
1. Pour the milk in the mixing bowl, cover it with a towel, and let it reach room temperature. If your bowl fits in the microwave, you could warm it up to room temperature more quickly that way. If you boiled the milk first, then let it cool to under 100 F degrees.
2. Once the milk in the bowl is somewhere between room temperature and 100 degrees, add in the plain yogurt with live cultures. You can use as much as you want, anywhere from a couple of tablespoons up to six ounces or so. Your yogurt will culture more quickly if you use more starter, but using more than a few ounces seems like a waste of money. If you are using powdered starter culture, then follow the label directions for quantity.
3. Mix in the yogurt with the spoon or spatula, trying to mash in any big clumps.
4. If using a different container for the yogurt, then pour the cultured milk into the container (beware: any remaining yogurt lumps will make splashes).
5. Cover the container with a towel. If the container has a lid, you can use this to cover it loosely, but a towel is great for allowing air circulation.
6. Follow specific directions for each of these different methods.

   Oven: Set the dial to the lowest possible setting, preferably 100 F degrees. If your lowest oven setting is 150 F degrees, then you can just turn on the oven for a few minutes until the temperature inside is around 100 degrees. Once the oven has reached the desired temperature (or you estimate it is pretty close), TURN OFF the oven, put the container of loosely covered, cultured milk inside, close the oven, and let it stay there overnight.

   Heating pad: There are different kinds of heating pads. If yours has a thermostat, set it to just under 100 degrees. If yours does not have temperature settings, then set it on medium heat. Cover it with a towel or a sheet of cardboard. Set the container of cultured milk on this, cover loosely, and let it sit overnight. This one will stay hotter than some of the others, so your yogurt might be done in as little as six hours.

Crock pot or slow cooker: Your quart-sized container may fit in here and it may not. If not, you may need to use a series of smaller container like small glass jars, drink glasses, or ceramic cups. Turn your crock pot on low heat for a few minutes, just until it feels warm to the touch, then turn it off, place containers of cultured milk inside, and cover with a towel or with the crock pot cover. If you are able to return and heat it up again the same way (on low for just a few minutes before turning it off again), then you will keep the internal temperature warmer. You can do this any number of times, whenever it has cooled to room temperature again. If you are asleep, this is harder to do, so you will just need to be patient while your yogurt takes a little longer to finish.

Warm water bath: For this method, you need to use a large pot wrapped with a large towel. Or you could use a slow cooker or crock pot without turning it on. Fill a kettle or pot with water, heat it on the stove, and pour in the large pot or crock pot until the water is at least 2-3 inches deep. Let this water bath cool to about 100 degrees, place the container of cultured milk in it (loosely covered), and then cover the large container. Insulate it as well as possible by wrapping it with a large towel. This should hold the heat for long enough to get the yogurt off to a nice start.

7. Check your yogurt after 7-8 hours, tasting it with a clean spoon. If it needs more time and you like it sour, give it 10 or even 12 hours. If you are trying a room temperature ferment, then it may need even longer. Once your yogurt is done, cover the container, refrigerate it, and eat/drink it at your leisure or blend it into smoothies!

Chapter 4: Rejuvelac

Before we get into more complex cultures, here is another one that's almost as simple to make as yogurt. Rejuvelac is a fermented beverage made from sprouted cereal grains, such as wheat, barley, rye, oats, triticale, millet, amaranth, quinoa, brown rice, wild rice, or buckwheat. It can be ready in 3-4 days.

You can use yogurt whey (the liquid from yogurt) or naturally occurring yeast and bacteria to ferment it. People have been making fermented drinks with grains for thousands of years, but the raw food advocate Ann Wigmore is credited with popularizing rejuvelac as part of a holistic health diet.

Rejuvelac is pretty sour, tasting much like the liquid whey from plain yogurt, so on its own this drink is an acquired taste. As with plain yogurt, you are welcome to add other flavors and sweeteners to rejuvelac. Personally, I can't drink it plain without gagging, but it becomes a lot more palatable if you add some sweetener after the ferment, such as fruit juice, maple syrup, or honey. Rejuvelac also makes a simple and effective fermented base for sodas or smoothies. This is a very healthy probiotic and quite easy to make.

First, you need some whole grains. Wheat, barley, oats, and rye are usually the cheapest and easiest to sprout. Even with the best of strainers, the small seeded grains, such as millet, amaranth, and quinoa, become pretty difficult to wash without losing some down the drain. I recommend using only organic grains if you can find some, because you will know they are free of any pesticides. Besides damaging your body, such chemicals may interfere with the fermentation.

You can either buy sprouting seeds, such as the hard red winter wheat that is generally grown to make wheatgrass juice, or you can just get some grains from a bulk bin at your local health food store. As long as you can find whole grains that are fairly fresh (which you can only confirm by trying to sprout them), then they should germinate reliably. It will take 1-2 days to sprout the grains. For a more comprehensive guide to sprouting raw foods, I recommend my short book *How to Sprout Raw Food: Grow an Indoor Organic Garden with Wheatgrass, Bean Sprouts, Grain Sprouts, Microgreens, and More*, which is available in e-book and print editions on Amazon.

Making Rejuvelac
Recipe makes one quart

Required materials:
One glass jar (a quart-sized Mason Jar works well)
Strainer, cheesecloth, or a sprouting lid for the jar
One large container (large enough to hold two quarts of liquid, glass or plastic)

Ingredients:
Half cup of whole grains
Water

Process:
1. Rinse the grains. Put them in the jar and cover with water. Let them soak overnight.
2. In the morning, drain the water from the grains, rinse them, and put them back in the jar.
3. Rinse the grains at least twice a day to prevent mold. Continue this for 1-2 days until you see little sprout tails on each of the grains.
4. Rinse the grains one more time and put them in the large container. You could use the same jar if it's big enough. Make sure to clean it well before using it again.
5. Cover the grains with one quart of filtered (non-chlorinated water).
6. Optional: Add a couple of tablespoons of yogurt whey (the liquid from some good quality yogurt). This provides the culture necessary to ferment the beverage. If you use whey, it will ferment more quickly, probably in 1-2 days. Without this, you will need to wait for the natural yeasts and bacteria to proliferate, which may add another day or two to the fermentation time.
7. Cover the container loosely. A loose lid, a towel, or cheesecloth works well. Place the container in a quiet place away from direct sunlight. Every 24 hours, use a clean spoon to taste it. The Rejuvelac should taste sour like yogurt. The ferment may take from 1-3 days depending on the temperature and strength of the culture.

8. Once it is ready, strain the rejuvelac into bottles or jars to cover and refrigerate. The spent grains can go in your compost. The best part of them is left in the water for you to drink. You can dilute it or add some fruit juice, maple syrup, or honey to make it tastier. Or use it as a base for the smoothies and sodas mentioned later in this book.

Chapter 5: SCOBIES: Ancient and Modern

When it comes to fermenting food, yogurt and rejuvelac are on the beginner level. When you enjoy making and consuming either one of these, your journey into fermented foods has only just begun. Beyond yogurt, there are many more healthful foods and beverages made with probiotic cultures. Most of these use a more complex array of cultures, but are still simple to make.

SCOBY (plural: SCOBIES) stands for Symbiotic Colony of Bacteria and Yeasts. While yogurt is fermented with a few selected bacterial strains, many other fermented foods use a complex mother culture of bacteria and yeast. In particular, a number of fermented beverages (kefir, kombucha, and naturally fermented sodas like ginger) are made by culturing the base ingredients with a SCOBY. Most makers of high quality vinegars use an ancient culture as well, known as the "mother" of vinegar. Though their compositions can vary somewhat, each SCOBY is a remarkably stable group of beneficial probiotic organisms.

Ancient SCOBIES

Most SCOBIES are truly ancient colonies of organisms. They have been handed down to us through the centuries so that every culture forms a living chain through human history. For thousands of years, people have continued to culture the same sets of bacteria and yeast by taking a bit of the culture, feeding and growing it, and then dividing it to share again. Your drink might be fermented with a culture used by the Apostle Paul, the Prophet Muhammad, Marco Polo, Catherine the Great, or Japan's samurai warriors.

The term SCOBY is generic. Depending on the fermented beverage and the origin of its culture, a particular kind of SCOBY usually has another name, too. For example, kefir cultures are called kefir grains, kombucha cultures are often known as mushrooms, and the ginger beer SCOBY is known as the ginger beer plant or ginger bug. Actual grains and mushrooms are not used, but these terms describe the appearance of the SCOBY cultures: kefir grains look like wet popcorn, while kombucha cultures form globular strands that must have reminded someone of a mushroom. Some of the bacteria in SCOBIES actually can be used to make synthetic leather. Here is a picture of a SCOBY mushroom and some kombucha fermenting equipment (note: some purists use only non-metal strainers and utensils to avoid imparting any electric charge to the culture).

Modern SCOBIES

In reality, you do not need to rely on centuries-old SCOBY cultures if you'd like to experiment creating your own. There are plenty of natural bacteria and yeasts on the leaves of cabbage plant, on the skins of grapes and apples, and even in the air in your kitchen. Whether you are fermenting beer, wine, sourdough bread dough, or any of the fermented foods mentioned in this book, "wild" yeasts and bacteria can get the job done.

You may be horrified even to consider fermenting food without first boiling and sterilizing all the equipment. But before you get out that antibacterial hand cleaner or slather everything with bleach, consider that we live in harmony with these small organisms. While *salmonella* and *e. coli* are among them, the presence of so many beneficial and benign organisms keeps the dangerous ones in balance. The bad guys only become a problem when the good guys get decimated and the balance shifts in their favor. Pathogens are much less likely to take over when you eat naturally fermented foods and encourage a rich array of beneficial microorganisms to thrive in your digestive system.

Some years ago, a fermentation advocate named Sandor Ellix Katz wrote a book called *Wild Fermentation*. Since then, he has written other books, including the bestselling *Art of*

Fermentation (which includes a forward by Michael Pollan). I am still indebted to Sandor for providing a nice review for my first book, but that is not the reason I am plugging his work.

Wild Fermentation is a manifesto, memoir, and guide for anyone who wants to ferment foods (particularly his signature sauerkraut) using yeasts and bacteria that are naturally present. The premise of the book is that you can ferment almost anything without adding starter culture: just prepare the base ingredients, let them sit, and in some cases continue adding more material to provide a steady food supply for the growing culture. If you build it, the yeasts and bacteria will come and do their job of fermentation, whether they were present on the cabbage leaves, inside of the pot you used, or even in the air itself.

Relying on wild fermentation gives you an opportunity to create your own modern SCOBY that is unique to your local environment. I would never use wild fermentation on milk products, since they can spoil at room temperature before a strong culture of beneficial organisms is able to build up a population. But I've used wild fermentation before to make sourdough bread, water kefir, sauerkraut, and ginger beer. San Francisco sourdough bread starter was created using a wild organism present in the air there (most people assume the starter uses a yeast, but it is actually a type of lactic acid bacteria). Many winemakers do not add yeast, but trust their fermentation to the wild yeasts that are naturally present on grape skins.

As long as you're willing to be patient and let the culture develop (which can take a few extra days), wild fermentation works just fine. And ironically, your culture may end up pretty similar to an ancient SCOBY, though probably not as stable or complex. It will contain some of the most common organisms, including natural wild yeasts, lactic acid bacteria, and acetobacter. Pretty quickly, the acidic, anaerobic environment that develops in your cultured food should prevent mold and other contaminants from taking hold.

And in a short time, the beneficial organisms will ferment your food. I cannot guarantee 100% safety from wild fermentation, which people with compromised immune systems may wish to avoid, but our ancestors have been using similar methods for most of human history and our bodies are well adapted to eating fermented foods. If the idea of unsanitized, wild fermentation makes you queasy, then feel free to boil all your equipment first and then start with a stable SCOBY that has evolved over a longer period. There is no shame in using either method.

How to Start Your Own SCOBY

Here is how to make your own SCOBY from store-bought kombucha. If you have a local health food or grocery store that sells raw kombucha, then buy a bottle of it and use this as your first starter. If you cannot find it locally, order some online. Try to choose a mostly plain kombucha as your starter, rather than one with a bunch of fruit juice or chia seeds mixed in. And it absolutely must contain live cultures, since sterilized kombucha has no value as a starter.

Take a sterilized quart or gallon jar or pitcher, pour in at least eight ounces of the kombucha, and add some room temperature sweet tea to the jar. You can make the sweet tea in advance from black, oolong, or green tea, plus one tablespoon of sugar per each eight ounces of tea. Cover the jar with a towel and secure it with a rubber band. Let the beverage ferment, which can take up to

2-3 weeks. As you watch it, you will see a SCOBY mushroom begin to form on the top; once it is ¼ inch thick or so, you can take it out and serve the remainder of this drink.

Chapter 6: Alcoholic Content of Fermented Beverages

If you are avoiding alcohol, have a particular health condition, are taking a medication with which it might interfere, or are planning to drink a large quantity of fermented beverages before driving, please be forewarned that the low level of alcohol in these drinks could cause you ill effects. I discourage you from drinking fermented beverages in any of these situations. You are solely responsible for investigating any potential issues related to the alcohol in fermented drinks, making yourself aware of the consequences, and taking the proper precautions.

Most of the time, homebrewed kefir, ginger beer, and kombucha should have an alcohol content of no more than 1% (and usually less than 0.5%). But this percentage could be a bit higher under certain conditions. Most of us would like to keep the alcohol level fairly low. By using less sugar, encouraging air circulation during fermentation, and harvesting your beverage earlier rather than later, you should be able to ensure the alcohol stays as low as possible.

I mention this because some people have an aversion to alcohol in any form or amount. But even juice that sits around has trace amounts of alcohol; it is part of the natural process. In drinking kefir, kombucha, ginger beer, and other cultured beverages, I have never felt any sort of alcoholic buzz myself. I cannot even imagine what a huge quantity of this stuff you would need to drink for it to result in a blood alcohol content (BAC) that could impair your driving. But it is always best to be cautious and consume raw, fermented beverages in moderation.

If you would like to INCREASE the amount of alcohol in your fermented beverages (and assuming that you are of legal drinking age), then use either kefir grains or ginger beer plant as your cultures. (Kombucha culture contains more acetobacter, which are capable of converting alcohol to acetic acid, so it is difficult to raise the alcohol level.) With kefir grains or ginger beer plant culture, you may be able to achieve a 1-3% alcohol content if you use lots of sugar, ferment for a longer period (and perhaps in multiple stages) and keep the culture going in a tightly sealed container. Be careful of the air pressure release when you open it. And drink responsibly.

Of course, if alcohol is what you're really interested in, then you probably should just culture your drink with brewer's yeast and follow directions from a good home brewing manual to give you higher quality stuff. I love drinking an occasional beer, wine, or alcoholic cider myself. But this book is more about making non-alcoholic fermented drinks or those with just trace quantities of alcohol.

Chapter 7: Kefir

Kefir is yogurt's grown-up cousin, fermented with a SCOBY culture called kefir grains. Milk kefir tastes a lot like yogurt, but it is a more powerful and concentrated probiotic. While yogurt cultures are not capable of colonizing your digestive tract in any meaningful way, kefir can help replenish the beneficial micro flora in your body. Most yogurt contains only four strains of beneficial bacteria, but kefir grains typically include some 30 types of beneficial bacteria and yeasts. Studies have shown these additional strains may provide more health benefits.

Kefir grains are most commonly used to ferment dairy milk and create the drinkable beverage known as kefir. They also can be used to create "water kefir", which is made from sugar water. Sugar, maple syrup, molasses, fruit juice, or another source of sweetener can provide enough fuel for the organisms to create a fermented drink. Milk kefir grains look like fluffy white popcorn or cheese curds, while the grains used for water kefir (also known as "tibicos") look more like translucent shavings of ice. Here are two pictures, the first showing milk kefir grains and the second showing water kefir grains.

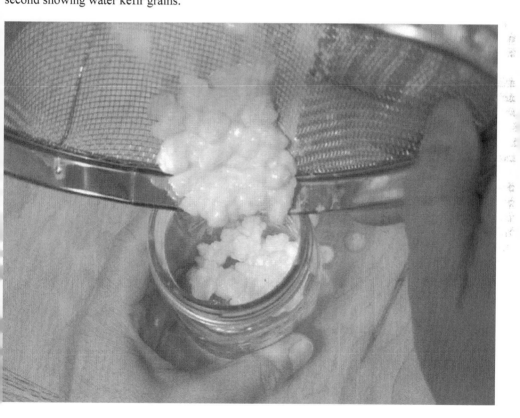

The drink has a long history. It originated in the Caucasus region, which extends from southern Russia down through Georgia, Azerbaijan, Armenia, and Eastern Turkey (kefir means "feel good" in Turkish). According to legend, kefir was a gift from the Prophet Muhammad to the people there. It seems likely that kefir was created by storing milk in goatskin pouches; either the Prophet or herders in the region discovered that culturing the milk extended its shelf life. Kefir's popularity extended to the Balkans on the other side of the Black Sea.

By the 13th century, fermented milk was important enough in the region that it was well known in Arabic medicine and documented by Marco Polo in his journeys through the land of the Tartars. The kefir culture was a closely guarded secret for many years, which Russians finally succeeded in capturing centuries later. There are stories of an elaborate plot to separate Ossetian tribesmen from their kefir grains in the early 1900s, once the Russian dairy industry recognized the potential of kefir.

The plot reportedly involved a beautiful Russian woman named Irina Sakharova, who was an employee of the Blandov brothers' dairy concern. She was sent to befriend the tribe's chieftain, Bek-Mirza Barchorov, who refused to give her any kefir grains but tried to marry her. Upon her departure, the chief kidnapped the woman, but her forced marriage was prevented when Russian agents rescued her. The chieftain was later hauled before the Russian Czar's court. Between a rock and a hard place, he was forced to give up his kefir grains.

Once the Russians succeeded in obtaining the culture, kefir spread rapidly in Russia, Eastern Europe, China, and beyond. Many Russians drink it every day. People in the Caucasus region, where kefir and other fermented beverages are widely consumed, enjoy some of the longest life spans on the planet.

Obtaining Kefir Grains

You can buy a dry, powdered culture for making kefir, but it lacks the strength to make more than one batch. The only way to keep your costs low and get the maximum probiotic health benefits from your kefir is to obtain some kefir grains. These grains are a community of beneficial bacteria and yeasts which began with an original mother culture.

By starting with a piece of that original mother culture, you can not only brew one batch of kefir, but continue to create an endless number of batches the rest of your life. Your supply of kefir grains will keep growing as you feed them (with milk for milk kefir grains, or with sugar water for water kefir grains). You will have enough culture to ferment your own drinks, plus extra grains to give away or sell to others.

The best way to get grains is to find someone in your area who will share them. A tablespoon or two is all you need. While milk kefir grains can culture sugar water and water kefir grains can culture milk, it is best to obtain the kind you plan to use, since that is the ultimate purpose for which these grains are best adapted. Your source of kefir grains must be someone you can trust, because your grains conceivably could be contaminated if the person did not take good care of them. It is pretty rare to have any meaningful contamination, though; the SCOBIES in kefir grains have proven to be remarkably stable over time.

If you cannot find a good local source, then order some kefir grains online. Both eBay and Amazon have a number of independent sellers offering kefir grains. Stick with sellers who have a lot of positive feedback, as this helps show their cultures are of good quality. Or check with your local chapter of the Weston A. Price Foundation. This organization is dedicated to promoting nutritious foods including ferments; your local chapter may have some members willing to share cultures with you. Again, avoid the powdered direct set cultures unless you just want to taste kefir once to see if you like it (hint: it tastes a lot like yogurt). The powdered starter is not strong enough to serve as a continuous culture as kefir grains can.

How to Make Milk Kefir

This is the fun part, and it's pretty easy. Just put one tablespoon of kefir grains in a cup of milk, and it will ferment at room temperature. I usually cover the cup or jar with a cloth to keep out any dust. Your kefir may be ready to drink in less than 12 hours, or in cooler temperatures it may need more time. You can speed this up by using more grains (say, two tablespoons) or slow it down by adding extra milk.

There are no rules about exactly when you need to stop. Feel free to taste your kefir along the way, since that is the best way to know if it is ready. If you like your kefir mild, stop the process a bit early, or keep on going for a stronger, "sour yogurt" flavor. Of course, you can always adjust the taste and sweetness after the fermentation by adding a bit of juice, jam, honey, maple syrup, or fresh fruit. Here is a recipe for making one quart of milk kefir.

Milk Kefir

Recipe makes one quart

Required materials:
One large mixing bowl (glass, plastic, or wood, but not metal)
Two glass jars (quart-sized Mason Jars are good)
One silicon spatula or wooden spoon
One plastic strainer
Cheesecloth, towel, or a sprouting lid for the jar

Ingredients:
One quart of milk (NOT ultra-pasteurized, which will not culture well)
One quarter cup (four tablespoons) of kefir grains
Optional: Dash of sea salt

Process:
1. Wash all equipment thoroughly before using.
2. Place kefir grains in the jar and fill it with the milk.
3. Optional: throw in a dash of sea salt, which adds trace minerals to support the fermentation.
4. Put the jar in an undisturbed place away from direct sunlight. Cover it loosely with the cheesecloth, towel, or a sprouting lid (which provides air circulation).
5. Check your kefir after 12 hours and again after 24 hours. Swish it around a little bit in the jar and then taste it with a clean spoon. If it's not sour enough for you yet, then give it another 12 hours. The fermentation will be faster in warm weather and slower when the air is cool. If you want to slow it down and fine tune your kefir, then you can put the whole jar in the refrigerator, where it will continue to ferment more slowly.
6. Once you are ready to stop the fermentation, use the strainer over a bowl to strain out the kefir grains from the beverage. Your kefir can be enjoyed immediately or stored in a jar or plastic container in the refrigerator.
7. See section below on Storing and Re-Using Your Kefir Grains.

How to Make Water Kefir

Water kefir is made by using kefir grains to ferment sugar water. Most people use brown sugar, cane sugar, or maple syrup, or another wholesome sweetener that provides more minerals than the depleted white sugar sold in stores. When the cultures do not have enough minerals available, they will not ferment effectively. Usually, water kefir grains (tibicos) are used to make water kefir, though milk kefir grains will work also.

Adding some sea salt (anywhere from a pinch to a teaspoon, depending on your preference) also can help ensure that minerals are present. Another option is to add some cut fruit or ginger to the ferment. This will supply a few more minerals as well as some flavor. But bear in mind that you will need to pick out the kefir grains later on from the fruit or ginger. And it is always possible to add flavor after the fermentation, once these grains are removed (see the chapter on making sodas for many post-fermentation flavor possibilities).

As an alternative to sugar water, you can use coconut water from a young coconut, which contains enough sugar and minerals that it does not need any added sweeteners or minerals. Young coconuts and coconut water are increasingly popular. You can find both of them at many health food stores as well as Latin American and Asian food markets.

Water Kefir (or Coconut Water Kefir)
Recipe makes one quart

Required materials:
One large mixing bowl (glass, plastic, or wood, but not metal)
Two glass jars (quart-sized Mason Jars are good)
One silicon spatula or wooden spoon
One plastic strainer
Cheesecloth, towel, or a sprouting lid for the jar

Ingredients:
One quart of filtered (non-chlorinated) water or young coconut water
One quarter cup (four tablespoons) of water kefir grains (tibicos)
Sweetener (not needed if using coconut water): One quarter cup of cane sugar, brown sugar, or maple syrup
Optional: Chopped or sliced fruit of your choice or sliced ginger root
Optional: Dash of sea salt

Process:
1. Wash all equipment thoroughly before using.
2. Place kefir grains in the jar, fill it with water, and gently stir in the sweetener.
3. Optional: throw in a dash of sea salt, which adds trace minerals to support the fermentation.
4. Put the jar in an undisturbed place away from direct sunlight. Cover it loosely with the cheesecloth, towel, or a sprouting lid (which provides air circulation).
5. Check your kefir after 12 hours and again after 24 hours. Swish it around a little bit in the jar and then taste it with a clean spoon. If it's not sour enough for you yet, then give it another 12 hours. The fermentation will be faster in warm weather and slower when the air is cool. If you want to slow it down and fine tune your kefir, then you can put the whole jar in the refrigerator, where it will continue to ferment more slowly.
6. Once you are ready to stop the fermentation, use the strainer over a bowl to strain out the kefir grains from the beverage. If you have used fruit or ginger also, you must pick out the kefir grains from these; my favorite tool for this is wooden/bamboo chopsticks. Your kefir can be enjoyed immediately or stored in a jar or plastic container in the refrigerator.
7. See section below on Storing and Re-Using Your Kefir Grains.

Storing and Re-Using Your Kefir Grains

Even when you are not using them, you can keep your kefir grains alive for future use. Basically, the procedure is to put them in a jar of milk or sugar water (depending on which type of grains you are saving), and then put this in the refrigerator. It will continue to ferment slowly, and the kefir grains should last for two weeks in the refrigerator. To keep them longer, first bring them out to conduct one kefir fermentation at room temperature, strain out the grains, and then return them to the refrigerator in milk or sugar water for another two weeks.

To save them for longer periods, it is also possible to freeze kefir grains. Wash them first with some clean water (to be sure, boil the water first and let it cool to room temperature). Strain the grains. Put them in a freezer container with enough dry milk powder (enough to cover them). Seal the container and place it in the freezer. You can store frozen kefir grains for up to two months.

Some sources also suggest it is possible to dehydrate kefir grains and rehydrate them. I would not do this because I worry about the effect on their long-term strength. If you're not going to make kefir for a couple of months, then I would suggest composting your grains or feeding them to pets (they are very nutritious). And then get some new grains when you are ready to begin fermenting again.

Chapter 8: Kombucha

Kombucha is a delicious beverage made by fermenting sweet tea. The tea is cultured with a SCOBY (SCOBIES were discussed in more detail in a previous chapter). The kombucha SCOBY is often called a "mushroom", perhaps because of its appearance or its historical confusion with a Chinese tea made from an infusion of tree fungus. For the base ingredient, you can use black tea, green tea, white tea, oolong tea, or a rarer variety, adding a little sugar or other sweetener to provide an energy source for the SCOBY culture. Of course, you are free to add any additional flavor you like, such as ginger, herbs, or fruit juice (flavoring is generally added after fermentation).

Like kefir, kombucha has a long history. This so-called "tea of immortality" was first recorded in China in 212 B.C. It may or may not be related to chaga, an ancient remedy made with an infusion of the healthful mushroom that grows on birch trees. A more likely scenario is that someone left out some sweet tea and forgot about it for a few days while it fermented. Or perhaps some ancient microbiologist deliberately invented kombucha.

Whatever its origins, Kombucha spread widely throughout the Eurasian trade routes and became firmly embedded in the culture of not only East Asia, but Russia, the Middle East, and much of Europe. It was introduced to Japan in 415 A.D., where it became a drink enjoyed by many. Most famously, it was the drink of the samurai warrior class.

The name is a bit of a mystery; some say the Korean doctor who brought the ancient elixir to the Japanese Emperor was named Kombu or Kambu. Others have speculated that the SCOBY mushroom may have looked like kombu seaweed, which is also made into a tea, and that foreigners may have confused the two brown liquids. In any case, this name seems to have come from Japan. The drink or its culture has also been known as Manchurian Mushroom, Tea Fungus, Japanese Sponge, Red Tea Mushroom (Japan), Wunderpilz (Germany), Elixir de Longue Vie (France), Tea Kvass (Russia), Volga Spring, Kargosok Tea, Tschambucco, Spumonto, Embuya Orientalis, and by at least a dozen other names.

While kefir culture is dominated by lacto bacteria, kombucha culture contains more yeasts and acetobacter. Both of these ancient SCOBIES seem to make beverages that are excellent probiotics and health tonics. One interesting fact about kombucha is that the acetobacter are able to turn ethanol (an alcohol) into acetic acid (like vinegar), so the alcohol content of kombucha usually stays pretty low.

How to Make Kombucha

To make kombucha, you simply mix up some sweet tea, put it in a jar, place your SCOBY in it, and cover it with a loose lid or a towel for aeration. Kombucha SCOBIES float near the top. For a quart of kombucha, use 2-4 tea bags and about one half cup of white sugar, which should be cooled to room temperature before you add the SCOBY. Yes, in the other chapters I recommend more wholesome sugars, but for kombucha, white sugar balances nicely with the tea.

Kombucha SCOBIES do not ferment as fast as kefir grains, so it probably will take from 1-4 weeks to brew a batch. The length of time varies based on the temperature, the SCOBY's potency, and your taste preference. As with other fermented beverages, you can drink it early at a slightly sweeter stage or you can let it ferment for a longer period for a stronger taste.

It's good to put your brew in a relatively warm place, where the air temperature is 65-82 F degrees (18-28 C degrees). Anything much colder than that may cause the yeast to shut down and go into hibernation. I find that the top of my refrigerator stays a bit warmer than room temperature. In colder weather, you can use a heating mat of the type used to grow seedlings.

Checking for Proper Fermentation

Your nose and the little bubbles should tell you if your kombucha is fermenting properly. But if you suspect something has gone wrong and the culture has failed, then you need to check it more closely. The best method of investigation is to use pH test strips. If, after 3-4 days of fermentation, the pH of your fluid is not in the 2.5-3.0 range, then it is not acidic enough and something has gone wrong. Dump it out, sterilize everything, and start again with a new culture. Also, if there is a strong kerosene smell coming from the kombucha, as opposed to a yeast or vinegar smell, that means something else has gotten in there and you need to dump it.

Fizzy Kombucha

If your kombucha is not as effervescent as you would like, you can conduct a secondary fermentation in a bottle. To fuel this second stage, you can use juice (which provides a nice flavor), or else use some more sweet tea. Either way, you will end up with a kombucha soda.

Take a plastic bottle with a tight-fitting lid, such as a soda or water bottle. (You can use a glass jar or bottle also, but it is easiest to check the air pressure in a plastic vessel.) Fill it three quarters of the way with your fermented kombucha and top this off with some additional juice. Tighten the lid and leave this at room temperature to continue fermenting. It probably will be ready in 2-7 days, but check it every day or so.

If you used a plastic bottle, then checking it is as simple as squeezing the sides of the bottle. If it has really puffed out so that squeezing is difficult, your drink should be ready. Open with caution, since the contents may be under pressure. Unless you've shaken the bottle, it really should not explode on you, but there will be a release of air pressure as there is when opening any soda bottle. Taste and decide if it's fizzy enough for you. If not, tighten the lid and give it another 12 hours or so.

Storing and Re-Using Your Kombucha SCOBY

Storing a kombucha SCOBY is easier than storing kefir grains, simply because it takes longer to ferment a batch. This means that you can start fermenting some sweet tea with a kombucha SCOBY and just leave it for as long as a couple of weeks. The fermented liquid may be undrinkably acidic, but your culture should still be alive after that time and you can begin using it again.

You can do the same thing and store the SCOBY in the refrigerator in its slowly fermenting beverage. The colder air will slow things down considerably and the yeasts may go dormant. The SCOBY should survive this way for a couple of months until you need it again.

Chapter 9: Ginger Beer

Ginger beer is another fermented beverage made with its own SCOBY. While you can make ginger beer with kefir grains or with another kind of SCOBY, a unique culture has evolved along with this drink. The culture is known as the ginger bug or the ginger beer plant (which, of course, is a SCOBY rather than an actual bug or plant). This culture is capable of making a drink with a higher alcohol content than some of the others mentioned in this book. It's a soda, it's a beer, and you can use as much ginger as you like for flavor and warmth.

Here is a picture of some naturally brewed ginger beer. With a lot of ginger, it can be pretty strong stuff. No problem; just use less if you prefer it milder.

In this chapter, we will discuss ginger beer using this SCOBY culture. The next chapter, which focuses on other naturally brewed ciders and sodas, also discusses making a ginger soda (which I call ginger ale). Basically, the terms "ginger beer" and "ginger ale" could mean the same thing. I have separated them only because the unique ginger beer plant culture deserves its own chapter (this one). The next chapter covers more generic sodas, including one I call ginger ale.

The ginger beer plant's origin is unclear; it may have come from India or Africa to the Caribbean, where it became popular in Jamaica in the 18th century. The ginger beer plant became widely used in Britain as well, which had breweries that exported a significant quantity of the beverage to the United States and Canada. In the late 19th century, a British biologist named Harry Marshall Ward began to collect and study the ginger beer plant culture.

Ward discovered that it was formed by the association of one type of yeast and one type of bacteria living in a harmonious SCOBY. The modern names for these organisms are *Saccharomyces florentinus* (which is the yeast) and *Lactobacillus hilgardii* (the bacterium). No one seems to know how the SCOBY ended up with just these two organisms, since other SCOBIES are more complex and diverse, but somehow the two seem perfectly balanced in terms of their needs and functions in the culture.

Here is another theory on how the ginger beer plant developed. The two organisms which make it up also can be present in water kefir grains. The ginger beer plant may have started as water kefir grains and then developed somehow into a less diverse culture. Perhaps temperature changes, inadequate handling, or too much ginger spice killed off the other strains. Whatever the case, the ginger beer plant SCOBY is as good as any other culture for fermenting not only ginger beer, but other sodas and drinks.

Once modern methods of brewing and bottling came around, the ginger beer plant faded into obscurity. Brewing and baking yeasts were easier to use and they could be added in powdered form rather than maintained as a living culture. The ginger beer plant almost went extinct. Germany and Jamaica were two of the only places where the culture was kept alive. Today, naturally fermented drinks have undergone a resurgence in popularity. There are now many individuals and small scale breweries that use this traditional SCOBY culture to make traditionally brewed ginger beer, though kefir and kombucha SCOBIES still are more widespread.

Ginger Beer
Recipe makes one quart

Required materials:
One large mixing bowl (glass, plastic, or wood, but not metal)
Two glass jars (quart-sized Mason Jars are good)
One silicon spatula or wooden spoon
One plastic strainer
Cheesecloth, towel, or a sprouting lid for the jar

Ingredients:
One quart of filtered (non-chlorinated) water
One quarter cup (four tablespoons) of ginger beer plant culture
One quarter cup or one half cup of sugar, preferably brown sugar, cane sugar, or maple syrup
1-2 inches of fresh ginger root, peeled and chopped
Juice of one lemon (vary amount to taste)
Optional: Dash of sea salt

Process:
1. Wash all equipment thoroughly before using.
2. Place ginger beer plant in the jar, fill it with water, squeeze in a little lemon juice, and gently stir in the sweetener.
3. Optional: throw in a dash of sea salt, which adds trace minerals to support the fermentation.
4. Put the jar in an undisturbed place away from direct sunlight. Cover it loosely with the cheesecloth, towel, or a sprouting lid (which provides air circulation).
5. Check your ginger beer every 12 hours or so. Swish it around a little bit in the jar and then taste it with a clean spoon. If it's not sour enough for you yet, then give it another 12 hours. The fermentation will be faster in warm weather and slower when the air is cool. If you want to slow it down and fine tune your ginger beer, then you can put the whole jar in the refrigerator, where it will continue to ferment more slowly.
6. Once you are ready to stop the fermentation, use the strainer over a bowl to strain out the kefir grains from the beverage. If you wish to reuse your ginger beer plant, you must pick

it out of the ginger; my favorite tool for this is wooden/bamboo chopsticks. Your ginger beer can be enjoyed immediately or stored in a jar or plastic container in the refrigerator. Alternatively, you can conduct a secondary ferment if you wish, which can build more carbonation and finish off the bottling. This process is described in the next chapter on ciders and sodas.

7. To store and re-use your ginger beer plant, please follow the directions used for kefir grains at the end of the kefir chapter.

Chapter 10: Naturally Cultured Ciders and Sodas

Root beer, ginger ale, and sparkling apple cider: what do these drinks have in common? All are sweet, sparkling beverages. And traditionally, all of them were brewed with probiotic cultures. In their natural form, these drinks retain far more goodness than your average soda pop. You can even call these drinks a health food.

Imagine a world with no high fructose corn syrup and pumped in CO_2 bubbles. Imagine sodas and ciders that are low in sugar, rich in protein and B vitamins, teeming with rich probiotics and enzymes, and naturally effervescent through fermentation. Plus, you can add whatever flavors and healthful herbs you want, making a custom soda to suit your tastes. If you've never tried cultured apple-blackberry cider, ginseng sarsaparilla, or lavender soda, you're in for a treat.

You can brew ciders and sodas using any of the cultures we have covered. Kefir grains, a kombucha SCOBY, a ginger beer plant, or even yogurt whey will get the job done. Of course, you can just use yeast if you want also, which creates more of an alcoholic beverage, since it does not have the bacterial component that breaks down alcohol into acid.

To keep a continuous culture going in juice or soda, my first choice would be kefir grains, specifically the kind used to make water kefir. Water kefir grains, which are adapted to culturing sugary water, will work the most quickly and have the best chance of maintaining a stable culture over time (assuming you plan to keep these grains after your first ferment). These grains can ferment a beverage in as little as 1-2 days, while a kombucha SCOBY will take up to 1-2 weeks.

Making Ciders (Cultured Juices)

The process of making ciders is extremely simple. Start with a bottle of your favorite juice (apple, grape, berry, etc.). Just open the bottle of juice or pour some into a jar for the fermentation. Then add your culture, which could be a kombucha SCOBY or a tablespoon or two of kefir grains, ginger beer plant, or yogurt whey. Then cover the bottle or jar loosely with the lid or cover it with a towel or cheesecloth, holding the latter in place with a rubber band. Leave the cultured juice in a place out of direct light where it can remain still for a few days.

Depending on the temperature and the strength of the culture you used, your cider might ferment in just a day or two. Stay on the lookout for little air bubbles forming. Feel free to pour off a little bit to taste each day. Near the beginning, it will be sweet from the sugars in the juice, and as it ferments, the sweetness will turn sour from the conversion of sugars to acids. When the taste is agreeable to you, go ahead and drink it at any point. Here are ways to achieve different levels of flavor and body:

Sweet and Mild

The juice begins with a sweet and mild flavor, so if you want to culture this lightly and get very little fermented taste, then simply drink it within the first day or two.

Mildly Fermented

To achieve this taste, let it go a little longer. This may be 2-3 days with kefir grains and a bit longer with other cultures. Taste it once a day until it has the fermented flavor you like, but still a bit of sweetness.

Strongly Fermented

Let it go an extra day or two for the most concentrated probiotic benefits. This is the strong, sour taste of a heavily fermented beverage. Your cider will have a bit of alcohol (probably under 1%) and should have the effervescence of a little natural carbonation.

Sweet and Sour

It's a cider, not a medicine! To get the full probiotic benefits of complete fermentation, plus the sweetness that makes it enjoyable, simply take out a few ounces of juice at the beginning and save this in the refrigerator. Ferment the rest, and once it is nice and sour, strain out any kefir grains or SCOBY, and then mix in the reserved juice. Or you could just add a pinch of sugar or a spoonful of honey, maple syrup, or molasses at the end. Voila, sweet and sour, the best of both worlds!

Fizzy Bottling

If your cider is not fizzy enough, try bottling it for a secondary fermentation. Take a plastic bottle with a tight-fitting lid, such as a soda or water bottle. (You can use a glass jar or bottle also, but it is easiest to check the air pressure in a plastic vessel.) Fill it halfway with the fermented cider and top this off with some additional juice. Tighten the lid and leave this at room temperature to continue fermenting. It probably will be ready in 24 hours, but check it within 12 hours. If you used a plastic bottle, then checking it is as simple as squeezing the sides of the bottle. If it has really puffed out so that squeezing is difficult, it is probably ready. Open with caution; you could have a bomb on your hands! Unless you've shaken the bottle, it really should not explode on you, but there will be a release of air pressure as there is when opening any soda bottle. Taste and decide if it's fizzy enough for you. If not, tighten the lid and give it another 12 hours or so.

Saving Your Culture

When you pour off the juice, you can do so with a strainer to catch any kefir grains, ginger beer plant, or SCOBY. A kombucha SCOBY sits on top of the liquid, so another way to catch it is to grab it with tongs. These solid cultures can be saved for the next fermentation project (please see the section on How to Keep a SCOBY Going in Chapter 4, which also applies to kefir grains). Yogurt whey or dried cultures will dissolve in the juice, so you can just drink it all or save a few ounces to mix with the next batch.

Using an Air Lock

Home brewing supply stores sell a very cheap device called an air lock (sometimes known as a water lock or pressure lock). This is a plastic valve with a rubber gasket that fits over the mouth of a bottle. There are some different styles (three piece, S-shape, and bubble locks), but they work the same way. You mount the device on the bottle that contains your brew, often with the help of a rubber stopper or bung that has a hole to fit the lock, then you fill this lock with a small amount of water. Some people prefer to use an alcoholic liquid, such as gin or vodka, instead of water. Here is a picture of an S-type airlock.

This liquid stays in the lock; it will not fall into the brew below. Once filled, the lock permits air to escape from the brew. Specifically, the carbon dioxide produced by the yeast or bacteria in your culture builds up enough pressure inside the bottle that it wants to come out. It will bubble up through the liquid in the lock. But the liquid will prevent any outside air, dust, mold spores, or insects from getting into the brew.

You do not need an air lock. A loose fitting lid will get the job done, too. But air locks make your job easier and help prevent any contamination. Plus, they are very cheap, with a set of three costing around the same price as a sandwich. You can find a good selection of them on Amazon or at any store that supplies home brewing equipment.

Making Sodas

Home-brewed sodas are awesome. They are far, far healthier than any high fructose, artificially flavored, chemically carbonated soda on the market. And making your own soda gives you the freedom to add any flavor you like. If you like root beer, cherry cola, ginger ale, cream soda, sarsaparilla, or lemon-lime, you can make it at home.

You can even make sodas that you'll rarely (if ever) find in any store. How about cranberry, apricot, mint, almond, pumpkin pie, or maple soda? Maybe pumpkin pie soda is not your cup of tea, but I'm trying to illustrate how much freedom you have. You can make soda with ANY KIND of flavor you like! Peanut butter, dill, peppercorn, chamomile, licorice, green tea? Okay, I'll stop. There are no limits.

Making your own natural soda is a three stage process. First, you will brew up the fermented base, which can be either kombucha, water kefir, rejuvelac, or ginger beer. Alternatively, you can just use brewer's yeast or baker's yeast. Of course, these single culture yeasts do not have the probiotic benefits of the traditional cultures described in this book.

Second, you will add some flavoring to this fermented base. Juices, fruit syrups, and herbal extracts are good flavoring candidates. Below the soda recipe that follows, you will find a list of flavoring sources, which include fruit syrups and juices, extracts of herbs and spices, and ready-made natural flavoring extracts such as cherry cola or cream soda flavoring. Third, you have the option to conduct a secondary ferment to add some carbonation and finish off the bottling of your soda.

The full process is described below.

Naturally Cultured Soda
(A list of flavoring sources appears below this recipe)
Recipe makes slightly more than one quart. In addition to the materials and ingredients needed to make water kefir, kombucha, rejuvelac, or ginger beer (which are explained in the chapters covering each of these drinks), you also will need some plastic bottles or jars with tight-fitting lids. Soda or water bottles with screw top lids work well. It is easier to check the inside pressure of plastic bottles by squeezing them, but you could use glass bottles or Mason jars and just take a small risk that they might blow up. If you use extracts for flavoring and still want to do a secondary ferment, then you should also have some extra plain tasting fruit juice (such as apple juice), fruit syrup, or maple syrup ready to add to each bottle.

Ingredients:

One quart of fermented base, such as water kefir, kombucha, rejuvelac, or ginger beer
Soda flavoring (see list that follows this recipe)
Extra juice, maple syrup, or fruit syrup

Process:

1. Make a batch of water kefir, ginger beer, kombucha, or rejuvelac as your fermented base for the soda. Please refer to the directions in the separate chapters on each of these. Bear in mind that kombucha will be the slowest among them, while the others are all pretty fast cultures.
2. Once you have made the base (following the directions in the appropriate chapter), pour it into each of the bottles or jars. Leave enough room for the fruit juice/syrup and any flavoring you wish to add.
3. Put the lids on tightly. You can leave the soda bottles out and check them every few hours or put them in the refrigerator, where they will keep fermenting more slowly. Kombucha soda should be left out.
4. Check your sodas by squeezing the sides of the plastic bottles. Once they are firm with the expanded pressure from the ferment, open them and taste. If you use glass bottles or jars, you will need to open them to check the fermentation. Beware of the pressure inside, which will release when you open the bottle. Once you taste the soda, only you will know when it is ready. If should be nicely fermented and effervescently carbonated, yet still sweet enough for you. If it's not strong enough, put the lid back on and let it ferment a few more hours. If it's too sour, add a little more of your juice or syrup.
5. Drink it and enjoy! Even the kids should love it!

Soda Flavoring Sources

Fruit Syrup: Any fruit or berry can be made into a fruit syrup, which combines with the fermented base to make a great soda. Soft fruit such as berries, grapes, peaches, apricots, cherries, plums, figs, and mangoes make particularly good syrups. Fresh fruit is best, but you can rehydrate dried fruit to make an effective syrup as well.

Take about two pounds of your favorite fruit, wash it, and chop it (except for berries and small fruit, which do not need to be chopped). Remove the pits from any stone fruit you use. Do not worry about the seeds in grapes or berries, since the syrup will be strained later. If the fruit you use is purely sweet and does not have any tartness to it, you can add some lemon or lime juice to balance this if you wish.

Put the fruit in a pan, adding one cup of water and one cup of sugar. Brown sugar, turbinado sugar, or cane sugar are best because they provide more minerals than white sugar. Cook the fruit on medium high heat, stirring it regularly and adding more water as needed to prevent sticking and burning. After 15-20 minutes, the mixture should look like a soupy jam. If any chunks remain, try to mash them in.

Let the fruit mixture cool, then strain it into a bowl or container. This is your fruit syrup, which can flavor any soda. If you have a lot of it, you can store it in a bottle or jar in the refrigerator for a few days. For longer storage, put it in the freezer in a freezer safe container. You can also follow a standard canning procedure used for jam, preserving the syrup in jars for whenever you need it.

Ginger Syrup for Ginger Ale: You probably will not need as much of this to get the flavor you want. Nevertheless, to make a great ginger ale, follow the direction above for making a fruit syrup, using fresh ginger root instead. Peel it, chop it, and boil it with some water and sugar to make a strong, tasty, healthful soda flavoring.

Fruit Juices: Juices can be used to flavor sodas as well. Grape, apple, and cranberry juices are good bets, and you can experiment with any others you like. In general, the more intense flavors are best. For example, dark purple grape juice has a great flavor, while some of the transparent, filtered apple juices just taste like sugar and water. Then again, there are really good apple juices that have full flavor as well.

Extracts of herbs and spices: Mint, lavender, and chamomile are three examples of herbs that make nice flavor additions in any soda. Then there are spices such as cinnamon, cloves, allspice, and curry, which might make interesting additions to a beverage. Please see the last section of this book for Lavender Soda and Pineapple-Cinnamon Tapache recipes.

There are several different ways to get herbs and spices into your drinks. With cinnamon, you can just put a cinnamon stick in for awhile. With fresh or dried herbs such as mint or lavender, you can boil them into any fruit syrup, or skip the fruit and just boil the herbs in sugar water to make herb syrup. With mint and chamomile, another option is to use herb tea bags for an herbal infusion. If you steep them in boiling water for awhile, then this tea water can be used to make syrup or simply added to the soda with as much sweetener as you want.

Ready-Made Flavoring Extracts: You probably have vanilla extract in your cupboard already. On the same shelf in the supermarket where vanilla is sold, you can usually find almond, peppermint, and coconut extracts. There may be a few more as well. You will need to experiment with the quantities until you find the right taste. In addition, you can order soda flavorings online (try an Amazon or Google search)for root beer, cola, cream soda, and more. If you don't find what you need from those specific links, there is a large selection on this site as well. Follow directions on each product label for using the proper quantities of these flavoring extracts.

Chapter 11: Probiotic Smoothies

Merriam-Webster Dictionary defines a "smoothy" (which I will spell as smoothie) as a beverage made from blending fruit with juice, milk, or yogurt. Smoothies are the healthier, fruitier cousins of the artery-clogging milkshake. They are an essential part of any raw or liquid diet.

I have been drinking smoothies since I was a kid, when someone blended milk with a banana. As an adult, the smoothies I make for my kids tend to be more complex than this, since we use a lot of different fruits and even vegetables in addition to yogurt or kefir. There are no rules for making smoothies, so my advice is to start with the information in this chapter and add whatever else you and your family might like to drink.

Smoothies even give you an opportunity to hide stuff that people DON'T like to eat or drink. For instance, I often sneak in small quantities of powdered vitamins, beet juice, kale juice, trace mineral drops, or nutritional yeast. What my kids don't know won't hurt them, and it may make them healthier.

Here are some of the elements of a smoothie and my suggestions of some ingredients that work well:

Liquid Base

Since a smoothie is a drink, it needs plenty of liquid. Any juice will suffice, but if you are blending in fruit as well, a juice-based smoothie gets pretty sweet. I often add some juice as a sweetener, particularly to balance out any sour yogurt, kefir, or fruit (see *Sweeteners*, below). But I rarely use juice as a "main ingredient" base because of all the extra sugar. Kombucha or water kefir can make a good, thin base as well. You can even use herb tea.

Most people like a creamy smoothie, which you can achieve by starting with a base of milk or milk substitute. Almond milk, rice milk, hemp milk, and soy milk are a few vegan alternatives. You can also use drinkable yogurt or kefir as a base, which will make a thicker smoothie. Any combination of the above is fine, too.

Thickeners

The best smoothies are thick like a milkshake. In my book, the two best thickeners are banana and solid (regular) yogurt. Drinkable yogurt and kefir will thicken while serving as a liquid base, but if you use another liquid as the base ingredient, then it's best to thicken with solid yogurt rather than drinkable yogurt.

Bananas are the secret to a good smoothie. They provide sweetness, creaminess when blended, and body to the drink. I am not much of a banana fan, yet I have never found a smoothie I liked which did not contain a banana. If you have other custardy fruit available in your area, such as a pawpaw or cherimoya, that might do the trick as well.

If you use enough soft fruit, it will thicken your drink. Ripe mangoes, strawberries, persimmons, and kiwis are good examples. Use enough soft fruit and you may not notice there is no banana! Just be aware that with kiwis and berries, using a lot of fruit makes for a seedy drink. Also, kiwis and milk do not go well together: the enzymes in kiwis are powerful enough to begin curdling the milk right away, which makes it bitter.

Melons and pears might tempt you as possible thickeners, but they are mostly water and tend to make the drink slushier rather than firmer (you are welcome to include them, but they will not have much of a thickening effect). I have yet to find a blender which can make a true puree from harder fruits like apples.

Often, I am tempted to add an extra banana or two for a thicker smoothie, especially if the other fruit I've used is not quite at its peak. I happen to think that a smoothie provides a great opportunity to use slightly sour fruit. For example, we may get some early season peaches that are not ready for prime time or some sour, under-ripe blackberries. These are great for smoothies, since the sweetness of a banana or two can balance the tartness of mediocre fruit.

Another option to thicken a smoothie is to use a dry powder or cooked grain of some sort. It must be something you like to eat/drink, because you'll need a lot of it. Protein powder, nutritional yeast, and cooked brown rice are some possibilities.

Sweeteners

If you use some tart yogurt or kefir and your fruit is not sweet enough to balance it, your smoothie might come out sour. This is when I might add an extra banana. Some other things you can use to add sweetness include honey, maple syrup, agave, stevia powder, fruit juice, or even a little jam. But beware of adding really acidic fruit juice (such as orange or cranberry juice) to an already sour beverage. Apple juice, grape juice, or even carrot juice are better as pure sweeteners.

Something Tart

Some smoothies get sweet without enough tartness to them. This can be the case if you use a lot of sweet fruit or store-bought yogurt. Some tart additions that add a good background flavor include oranges and other citrus fruits, orange juice, cranberry juice, or plain, sour yogurt, kefir, rejuvelac, or another cultured and unsweetened drink.

Something Cold

If you're conditioned to thinking of a smoothie as a milkshake or slushed ice drink replacement, then you might want it colder than room temperature or even fridge temperature. The best way to get that frosty thing going is to blend in some frozen fruit or frozen juice. You can freeze your own yogurt or kefir to blend in as well. During the height of fruit season, I find myself freezing a lot of strawberries, blueberries, blackberries, pitted cherries and apricots, and melon cubes. We pick them ourselves or buy them in bulk when the fruit is cheap, plentiful and at its peak. Then we use these frozen fruits all year long in cooked cereals, muffins, and other baked items. But mostly, they end up in smoothies. Before trying to make a frosty drink, make sure you have a good blender that can handle ice. Frozen bananas work well, too.

Aromatic Flavor Sources

Long ago, I became bored with routine smoothies. I like to taste the fruit in it. This is partly because I've usually added some kale juice or other vile tasting health ingredient that I want the kids to drink. The smoothie must be tasty enough they will want to drink a lot of it without knowing they are drinking their veggies too. Plus, it's nice to have a smoothie with a theme ingredient and a dominant flavor, though sometimes a mish-mash of various ingredients tastes good also.

If you have a black-and-white screen or print booklet, then you will not be able to see the brilliant color in the picture below. It is like the one on this book's cover, which you should be able to see on your computer screen. The smoothie is a vibrant bright purple and almost thick enough that a spoon would stand in it. You just can't beat the taste of wild blackberries, which make the most beautiful smoothie as well!

Examples of tasty, aromatic, and potentially dominant flavors include mango, pineapple, peach, apricot, strawberry, raspberry and blackberry. You can achieve any of these by adding a few handfuls' worth of the theme ingredient. If you can't taste it above the background of the smoothie, add some more and blend again, repeating this until that delicious flavor emerges above the background tastes. With most other fruits, such as apples, pears, grapes, melons, and plums, they are rarely aromatic enough to dominate a smoothie (though there are a few varieties of each which can add very strong aromas, such as Concord grapes and Santa Rosa plums).

Other Weird Ingredients

Growing up in California, I have always enjoyed avocadoes. However, I have never been able to accept avocadoes in sweet (as opposed to savory) dishes. In the Philippines, some people put sugar on avocadoes for dessert, and some gourmet ice cream shops sell avocado ice cream, but

I'm more of a guacamole or avocado sandwich/salad person. If you are not stuck on the same hang-up as I am, then an avocado would be a very nutritious, thickening addition to any smoothie.

I like to use vegetable juices in smoothies also. Carrot juice is easy to add, since it is sweeter than many fruits. Beet juice and pumpkin juice are pretty sweet too. I also juice my own homegrown kale, which I then freeze in ice cube trays. It is very easy to use a cube of this frozen kale juice in soups, bean dishes, omelets, and pastas. It packs a nutritional punch but is simple enough to hide. I won't put a whole ice cube of kale juice in a smoothie, but I will shave some of it in.

Since it is a lot of trouble to fire up both the juicer and the blender at once (and clean both of them up), I find that freezing the little ice cubes is a good way to go. I can juice a lot of vegetables at a time and only clean the juicer once. Then those little ice cubes of vegetable juice are ready whenever I need them.

There is no reason you can't add spices to your smoothie if you like a different flavor. Think of the carrot cake, pumpkin pie or apple pie spice thing. A little chocolate might be a good, too. Dare to try some cayenne pepper? I have juiced ginger root before and used a bit of this in a smoothie. If you have a really strong garlic press, like the kind that professional chefs use, you can use it to press ginger as well. After breaking several lesser models by trying to press ginger, I finally got a $30 garlic press instead of a $3 one. It has been pressing ginger for me for several years now.

Thinking outside the box, why not try a savory smoothie? These are also known as cold soups. Yogurt or kefir plus tomato juice with a little garlic and herbs sounds great. Or you could peel some cucumbers and puree them with yogurt or kefir, adding a little curry powder to make something approaching Indian raita. Starting with yogurt, kefir, or kombucha, try making your own probiotic take on a well known soup, such as raw Russian borscht, Spanish gazpacho, or Latin American ceviche. You might even find a use for avocadoes in a savory smoothie or cold soup.

Or just buy some readymade soup, blend it with yogurt or kefir, and eat it cold. If it's thick enough, you can call it a dip instead. There are lots of possibilities.

Chapter 12: Additional Recipes for Kombucha, Sodas, and Smoothies

In summary, I hope you have enjoyed this short book on making probiotic, cultured drinks. They are an important addition to any raw food or liquid food diet. In fact, they are a great addition to any diet, even if it's a burger and fries diet. Best wishes on your delicious and healthy journey into fermented drinks. I will leave you with a few recipes: for lavender soda, root beer, ginseng root beer, blackberry smoothie, and pineapple-cinnamon tapache. Some of them are my own creations or adaptations of recipes that I obtained long ago from some forgotten source. Other recipes below are available through web links; these are ones that I have enjoyed, but do not own, and are excellent enough that I could not improve upon them. Enjoy!

Lavender Soda: Works best with ripe soft fruit, such as mangoes, peaches, plums, or apricots. 1 cup water, ½ cup sugar, 2 tablespoons lavender flowers, juice of one lemon or lime, one pound of ripe fruit. Boil water, remove from heat, add sugar and lavender, and cover. Wash and chop fruit. Strain out lavender by pouring out sugar water through a sieve, pouring it over the fruit. Blend this fruit/syrup mixture or puree it in a food processor. Strain the puree until you have at least two cups of fruit syrup.

Either: (1) Ferment sugar water and then add some of this syrup to taste at the end, or (2) Pour syrup into a bottle or jar, and add about the same amount of water (e.g. two cups of syrup, topped by two cups of water). Add your culture, cover it loosely, and check it in a day or so. If it needs more fermentation, then give it another day. If it comes out too sour, add a little sugar or other sweetener. If it's not tangy enough for your taste, add some more lemon or lime juice.

Root Beer From Scratch (via Chow.com): http://www.chow.com/recipes/10681-chow-root-beer

Root Beer (or any other soda) the Simpler Way: Use ready-made root beer extract, which is available online.

Ginseng Root Beer: Boil fresh or dried ginseng root in water and let it steep for several hours. If you want a heavy hit of ginseng, then mash in the root or blend it. Use this water in your root beer recipe.

Blackberry Smoothie: 2 cups drinkable yogurt or kefir, 1 cup blackberries (fresh or frozen), 1 banana, ½ cup other soft fruit or ½ cup apple or orange juice. Put yogurt or kefir in the blender first, then the fruit. Blend until pureed and then drink. Makes one very large "meal" smoothie or 2-3 smaller ones.

An incredible list of **green smoothie recipes**: http://www.incrediblesmoothies.com/green-smoothie-recipes/

Pineapple-Cinnamon Tapache: This is a traditional fermented drink from Mexico, which has become one of my favorite quick fermented drinks. It involves cutting up a whole pineapple and fermenting it in water for a couple of days, along with some sugar and spices. This creates a concentrated drink that you can dilute with more water for a delicious and refreshing tropical beverage. You could also use another kind of fruit if you prefer, or you could adjust the quantities of spices to suit your taste preferences.

Traditionally, people placed the pineapple rind (skin) in the water also and just cultured the drink using the wild yeasts and bacteria that were present on the skin. You could try this (making sure there is no mold on the bottom of the pineapple rind). I prefer to use water kefir grains, which means there is no reason to leave the rind in the water (I give fruit rinds to my chickens, who peck them clean).

1 fresh pineapple, cut into cubes

4 quarts water (16 cups)
3 cups of brown sugar
1 cinnamon stick
Optional: 1 tablespoon apple pie spice (or 2 cloves)
1 teaspoon vanilla extract

Put the cut pineapple in a large container and cover with water (using about half of the water, or enough to cover the pineapple). Add the sugar, spices, and vanilla also. Add 1-2 tablespoons of water kefir grains, either loosely or suspended in the water in a cloth bag. Let it sit for a couple of days. After about 48 hours, add another quart of water, and let it sit for another 12 hours.

Then taste it using a clean spoon. If it tastes good, remove the fruit and kefir grains and pour the drink into bottles or into a clean container and refrigerate what you cannot drink. This will slow down the fermentation and give you a few days in which to drink it. If the drink is not ready yet (too sweet or too mild), you can add more water and give it another 12 hours of fermentation before cleaning and storing it as described above. At the end, if it's not sweet enough for you, add a little honey, apple juice, or sugar when you drink it.

Hopefully, this short book will help you open a new chapter in your enjoyment of fresh foods. Please feel free to drop me a line at the e-mail address listed on my Amazon author page. Also, if you have a moment, I would really appreciate it if you could write a brief review on there for this book. Your thoughts will help future readers. Thanks!

My Publications (all are available as Kindle e-books, with some also available as printed pamphlets)

(Click my author name on Amazon for more titles)

1. How to Sprout Raw Food: Grow an Indoor Organic Garden with Wheatgrass, Bean Sprouts, Grain Sprouts, Microgreens, and More

Grow Your Own Raw Food Anywhere!
Would you like to grow some of your own food this year? Indoors? With no sunlight or soil? At any time of the year and at all times of the year? Sprouts allow you to do all that and more. In fact, you can grow all the vegetables your body needs (plus all the protein as well) in an area that's no bigger than your microwave oven. I grow sprouts on top of my refrigerator, harvesting

askets of fresh, raw food every week without even going outside.

Growing sprouts is simple and it's cheap. Sprouts can provide you with the power-packed nutrition your body needs at a fraction of the price of store bought food. You can save money while eating right. There's no dirt, no pests, and no weeding required.

Contents Include:

1. Superfood Sprouts
Cheap, Easy to Grow, Provide Year-Round Nutrition

2. The Benefits of Raw Food
Lose Weight, Nourish Your Body, and Stimulate Energy Levels

3. Sprouting Equipment and How to Use It
Trays, Jars, Bags, Automatic Sprouters, and Wheatgrass Juicers

4. Salad and Sandwich Sprouts
Alfalfa, Clover, Radish, and Broccoli

5. Bean Sprouts
Mung Beans, Soy Beans, Lentils, Peas, and More

6. Grain Sprouts
Wheat, Barley, Rye, Oats, Triticale, Quinoa, and Other Grains

7. Seed and Nut Sprouts
Sunflower, Sesame, Pumpkin, Peanut, and Flax

8. Seasoning Sprouts
Basil, Celery, Cress, Dill, Fenugreek, Mustard, Onion Family, and More

9. How to Grow Microgreens
Grow a Gourmet Baby Salad, Anytime, Anyplace!

10. Wheatgrass Juice From Homegrown Sprouts
How to Grow and Juice Your Own Wheatgrass

11. Where to Get the Best Sprouting Seeds
Trusted Sources for the Freshest Quality

12. Where to Find the Best Raw Food Sprout Recipes
Delicious ways to enjoy your sprouts, raw or cooked

2. Backyard Chickens for Beginners: Getting the Best Chickens, Choosing Coops, Feeding and Care, and Beating City Chicken Laws

Description from Amazon:

Excellent booklet for beginners on how to start a backyard mini-flock of 2-4 chickens and get fresh eggs every day. Written by the author of the best-selling Fresh Food From Small Spaces book, a former columnist for Urban Farm magazine. (Updated 2012 Version)

Topics include:
• Fresh Eggs Every Day
• How Much Space Do You Need?
• Building or Buying a Coop
• Feeders, Waterers, Nesting Boxes, and Roosts
• Getting Chicks or Chickens
• Feeding Your Chickens
• Tips for Cold Climates
• Health and Safety
• Dealing with Neighbors, City Chicken Laws, and Other Challenges
• Resources: Everything You Need!

3. How to Grow Potatoes: Planting and Harvesting Organic Food From Your Patio, Rooftop, Balcony, or Backyard Garden

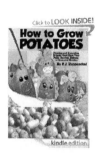

Description from Amazon:

Perfect beginners guide to growing potatoes. This booklet explains how to plant and grow organic potatoes for food in the home garden. Recommended for backyard gardeners and container gardeners with small city-sized yards, patios, balconies, decks, and rooftops.

• Why Grow Potatoes? Six Great Reasons

- Different Kinds of Potatoes (and Where to Get Them)
- Growing in Containers, Raised Beds, and Traditional Rows
- Planting and Hilling Potatoes
- Soil, Fertilizer, and Watering Needs
- Harvesting Potatoes
- Storing Potatoes for Later Use
- *Bonus*: Two Secret Tips for Getting More (and More Delicious) Potatoes

4. Blueberries in Your Backyard: How to Grow America's Hottest Antioxidant Fruit for Food, Health, and Extra Money

Description from Amazon:
Perfect blueberry growing guide for beginners. This booklet explains how to plant and grow blueberries in the home garden. Recommended for backyard gardeners with small city-sized yards, patios, balconies, decks, and rooftops. (Updated 2012 version)

Topics include:
- Why Grow Blueberries? Six Great Reasons
- Blueberries for Every Climate (and where to get them)
- Grow Blueberries Almost Anywhere: Doorsteps, Patios, Balconies, Rooftops, and Yards
- Perfect Blueberry Soil (regular garden soil kills them, but they will thrive in this!)
- How to Plant and Grow Blueberries in Raised Beds and Containers
- Feeding, Watering, and Caring for Your Blueberry Bushes
- Making Extra Money Growing Blueberries

5. Fall and Winter Gardening: 25 Organic Vegetables to Plant and Grow for Late Season Food
Description from Amazon:
Complete guide to growing organic vegetables for a fall and winter garden. This book explains which vegetables can survive in cold weather and how to grow them. Recommended for backyard gardeners and container gardeners who want to grow food for fresh eating all year round.

Topics Include

- Introduction to Late Season Vegetable Gardening
- 25 Vegetables for Cool Seasons
- Starting Vegetables From Seed
- When to Plant in Your Area
- Preparing the Soil and Fertilizing
- Garden Rows, Raised Beds, and Containers
- Extending Your Season
- Harvesting and Storing Your Produce
- Resources: More Information

Author Info

R.J. Ruppenthal is a licensed attorney and college professor who has a passion for growing and raising some of his own food. He is based in California, though he has experience trying to grow winter vegetables in Wisconsin. He regularly writes and blogs about fruit and vegetable gardening, growing food in small urban spaces, sustainability, and raising backyard chickens. On occasion, he even pens something about law or government. You can follow his blogs on his Amazon author page at http://www.amazon.com/R.J.-Ruppenthal/e/B00852ZTT2/ref=ntt_athr_dp_pel_1